SELL ON PURPOSE

LAMAR SKIPPER

Chapters

Description

No matter what product or service you sell, *Sell on Purpose* will set you apart and show you how to bring value to your market. *Sell on Purpose* will show you why it's so important to know your purpose and how knowing your purpose will help you succeed. *Sell on Purpose* was written to help those in sales increase their belief, passion, and purpose for what they do, which in turn will bring better results and more fulfillment in their experience. You will clearly see how you are the key to your success and *Sell on Purpose* will show you how to use this key to open the door to your next level and beyond.

Chapter 1 - What's your purpose

Sales over the years have occasionally been seen as a dirty word. A profession needed to move products and services; it rarely gets the respect or appreciation it deserves. In my opinion, sales are part of the foundation of a good and growing economy. They are essential! As I write this chapter, life on Planet Earth has changed, and a lot of uncertainty exists. COVID 19, a virus that seems to have started in China, has worked its way to America and is currently changing our way of life. Social distancing and working from home is quickly becoming our new normal. Regardless of how things change for us in the way we do business, sales in general will and have always been needed to move our economy forward.

No matter what business you are in, sales of the product or the service are an essential part of the process. My intention for writing *Sell on Purpose* is to help those in sales increase their belief, passion, and purpose for what they do, which in turn will bring better results and more fulfillment in the experience.

So, let me start by asking you a question: "What's your purpose?" Purpose has been defined as the reason for which something is done or created or for which something exists. To be more specific, why are you in sales, if that's your occupation? Or which process of the sale do you facilitate? You see, you are either in direct sales or you facilitate a process of the sale or the fulfillment of the sale or service. No matter what, these three things exist within the movement of every product or service. You are either making the sale, facilitating a process of the sale or fulfilling the sale or service.

This is important to know and understand because it keeps us focused on the purpose, which will increase our belief in the importance of what you do when you have an understanding of the importance of the purpose of what you do and a rock-solid belief in it that's a receipt for colossal success.

You may love service and helping people. Your passion may be for the development of new products or services. You could be driven by challenge or being the best at what you do or sell. Or you could be more intellectual in your approach, which leads you to have more focus on facts and figures.

You need to recognize what draws you to what you do at your core. You need to know your specific purpose for what you do and why you do it. Knowing your purpose will unlock excitement and energy for what you do, and it will help you to do it better and with more passion. Simply put, we need to go inside and find out what inspires you. What moves you, what excites you about what you do, and why! The why is the key that will help you to see your purpose clearly, and when you move with purpose, you Sell on Purpose!

When you Sell on Purpose, you unlock many benefits for you and your prospect. First, you're enthusiastic about your part in the process. You see your role as essential and necessary! You know the need for what you do and the benefits it provides. Second, you're passionate about the cause, also known as the mission. You see yourself and your opportunity as a part of a more substantial NEED! A need that you're helping to fulfill to your part of the world. You know what you do is more significant than you! Third, you're persistent! You go go go! You're all about action! Your focus is on what needs to be done, and you make no excuses! You have an I can, I will, I must mindset that gets things done in a way that makes others admire and naturally want to follow your lead! When you Sell on Purpose, you inspire everyone who comes in contact with you one way or another. They either love your enthusiasm, admire your passion, or they're amazed by your persistence. Your influence is magnetic when you Sell on Purpose!

1. What do you sell? Why is it a need? What happens if people don't have your product or service?_____________________

____
____
____
____
____

2. What's your level of belief in your product or service related to its benefits to your prospects (1-10 1 being they don't need it 10 being they shouldn't want to live without it)_________

____
____
____
____
____

3. Describe what you do in the form of a mission. Example - My mission is to educate homeowners about mortgage protection so they can protect their families from foreclosure due to death and illness. I will help as many people as I can because I wholeheartedly believe in what this product does._______

____
____
____
____
____
____
____
____

Chapter 2 - Why is the Key

In the first chapter, I stated that "The why is the key that will help you to see your purpose clearly, and when you move with purpose you Sell on Purpose." Your why is the key because it unlocks your vision for what you do and gives it meaning.

Knowing your why is the key to unlocking your energy, creativity, passion, enthusiasm, and your purpose. This is the internal stimulation that immensely affects everything you do, say, and think. Knowing your why and keeping it in front of you as your call to action puts you in a class all by yourself because it keeps you on target. It keeps you focused, and it allows you to access a never-ending supply of drive.

I recently listened to a video of David Goggles, an incredible example of what humans can achieve and accomplish when we remove all doubt and fear. His story of persistence is almost unbelievable and absolutely inspiring. In the video, he talked a little about the difference between drive and motivation. In that video, he mentioned motivation is crap but used a heavier word and said Drive is the Key! He talked about going inside and investing some time with yourself to tap into the Real You! In my personal experience, this is why finding your why is so crucial to your success and achievement. Finding out what inspires you and drives you to go further than you can even imagine and to demand more of yourself than anyone could ever expect is and always will be an inside job! You can't get there through outside stimulation. Reaching for the next big thing won't ever be enough to keep you growing and going! Accomplishment and achievement won't bring fulfillment and internal satisfaction. In my opinion, fulfillment and satisfaction come from doing what you know you're meant to do. It comes from living your purpose and knowing your why!

Dani Johnson, an incredible trainer inside the home base business industry, is absolutely amazing. I've seen her live several times and have personally benefited from her training and events. In her personality test, she talks about the four dominant personalities that we have as humans and how different factors drive each personality. The four are: emeralds, sapphires, rubies, and pearls. She says Emeralds are driven by facts and figures. Sapphires are driven by fun and excitement. Rubies are driven by challenge and goal achievement. And Pearls are driven by their need to help and be of service. She says everyone has one of these four as a dominant personality, and many have a secondary one as well. This information is extremely helpful in determining what drives you and understanding your why. If you want to access all the benefits of your unlimited resources, you must first find your Key.

This key is yours and yours alone. It can't be given to you, and it can't be taken from you either! It comes from the inside out and not from the outside in! Below are steps you can take to find your why and begin to use it to Sell on Purpose.

1. What are you driven by? Facts and figures? New challenges and accomplishments? Helping others and providing service? Having fun and experiencing new adventures?___________

____
____
____
____
____
____
____

2. How does what drives you, help you do what you do in your occupation? How do they relate to each other?___________

____
____
____
____
____
____
____

3. What fulfills you about what you do and why?___________

____
____
____
____
____
____
____

4.   Do you know why you do what you do in your profession?

____
____
____
____
____
____
____

5.   What's your why, and how can you fulfill it doing what you
     currently do?_________________________________

____
____
____
____
____
____
____
____
____

Chapter 3 - Purpose Driven Sales

Purpose is a word that's used more and more in the world today and rightfully so. Because it brings meaning and emotion into the conversation. When I say Purpose-driven sales, I'm mainly talking to that area of the product or service directly responsible for the sale of the product or service. Although these principles can be applied to all parts of the process and can help everyone involved, the individuals most responsible for the sale will be my primary focus for this chapter. We've already discussed some of the benefits of selling on purpose, so now let's talk a little more about why it matters to you and your success in the present and future. Whatever the current level of achievement and success you have obtained thus far, I want to go out on a limb and say you have barely scratched the surface of what's possible for you and the impact you can make. The reason I say that with absolute belief is simple, because you're reading this book! First, most people are rarely willing to learn and grow. By reading this and other books as I'm sure you have already, I would venture to say you're a seeker—a person who searches for more and who's driven already. Second, in my experience, those who seek usually aren't doing it for their immediate gratification. There is something inside of you that wants out, that needs to be expressed! What you're searching for you already have and what you need to express is waiting for you to believe in your value so it can be released. Third is just putting it all together and presenting it to the world.

Let's look at an example of this in the cooking industry. Let's say you have a passion for cooking, and you're always in search of new and amazing meals to cook. Your passion drives you, but what's the purpose, and where does it come from? We'll answer that question in a moment, but let's look at this in 3 steps. First, you search for a new and amazing dish to cook, and eventually, you find one that's amazing or you invent one yourself. Second, you get all the ingredients you need or think you will need, and you begin to put it all together. You work at it over and over and over again until it finally tastes amazing. Third, you present it to the world or maybe just your family and loved ones to start. And they love it! You're so excited, and you love how they have enjoyed what you have made. Now take a moment and look at the three steps involved in this process. First was seeking and searching. Second, was getting all the necessary ingredients together and putting them together until it tastes amazing. Third was presenting it to the world or your world. In this process, we see how someone's passion can come to life while moving them to action, how the sheer desire within them is expressed in time and calls for release. And in this example, by taking a closer look, we can see the purpose. The seeking alone revealed the desire, but to find out what the purpose is, we need more information about the person. We need to know some things about their past and why they started cooking in the first place. Finding out what cooking means to them will also help us to find their purpose. We also need to know their personality type, as stated in chapter 2.

Let's finish this example and answer all of these questions. Let's say this person grew up watching their mom and dad cook, and it was always an enjoyable experience. So over time, they connected cooking with fun and family time. Let's also say their personality type is sapphire, meaning they're driven by fun and excitement. Knowing all this, you can see this person's passion for cooking new and or inventing new dishes is driven by their purpose. Remember the definition of purpose; the reason for which something is done or created or for which something exists. This person is cooking because they enjoy the fun and excitement of cooking new dishes and or inventing them. In their childhood, they connected cooking to fun and family time. So as an adult, cooking is an expression of what's already inside of them that wants out and needs out. Cooking is their way of expressing who they are. So take all of that and apply it to you.

1. What do you use to express who you are? _______________

____
____
____
____

2. What gives you excitement and purpose? _______________

____
____
____
____
____
____

3. Is there a way to connect that to the product or service you
    sell? ____

____
____
____
____
____
____

4. What's your personality type? _______________________

____
____
____

5. How does all this fit together for you?_________________

____
____
____
____
____
____
____
____

Chapter 4 - What are you Selling & What are they Buying

To Sell on Purpose successfully, you must also know and understand what you're selling & what your prospect is buying. As I write this chapter, the majority of my country is on lockdown, and only people who are deemed essential are permitted to travel to and from work. Everyone else is advised to stay home and only travel if necessary. Entire industries have shut down, leaving millions of people instantly out of work and unemployed. I believe most, if not all, of these industries like bars, nightclubs, casinos, and dine in restaurants will open back up. But some of them won't recover, and the ones who do should see their business differently. In my opinion, even after COVID-19 has been beaten and all these restrictions lifted, businesses that were not deemed as essential should at least start to explore other ventures that are. Or new ways to deliver their product or service to the market. So that if a new pandemic rears its ugly head, they have an industry that's seen as an essential to fall back on or a way to continue their current business in a new pandemic.

If what you're selling is an essential need, then people will buy it because they feel like they need it; yet, I can assure you they have so many options, it's beyond belief when it comes to choosing that particular product or service. So what you're selling matters just as much as what people are buying. Both sit opposite and equal to your success in sales. So let's look at these two and see how they become one. First and foremost, when it comes to a product or service that's readily available and easily accessible, sales become more of a numbers game to the salesperson in most situations. Car insurance, for example, isn't really sold anymore because it's required by law, so companies just compete on price and accessibility. If you have reasonable rates and people know who to call when they're in need, you will do well. However, other products like life insurance must be sold because it's not against the law not to have it. 41% of all US households still doesn't have life insurance and half of the those households who have say they don't have enough (Reports LIMRA 2/2020). Whether you sell a product or a service that's seen as essential or not, or that is required by law to have or not, knowing what you're selling and what people are actually buying will put you in a class all by yourself.

People make decisions emotionally and justify those decisions rationally. The emotional side of the decision is made by salespeople who know what their prospect is buying and lost by salespeople who don't. And if you haven't guessed it yet, your prospect is buying You! Yes, You! Whether they trust you and believe you will be a significant factor in your sales success. So when you understand what your prospect is buying, you can then focus on selling the right thing. If everything is just about equal (and the internet has really helped with that), making products and services readily available, your prospect will act on an emotional decision as soon as they hear or see something that makes them feel good about that emotional decision. This gives them enough information for them to defend that decision rationally if need be. Since you are the key to your own success in sales, you have to work on yourself on the inside to get the best outside results. Selling on purpose will give you the why and meaning for what your selling. It will help you harness all the benefits that come along with knowing your purpose and moving with it. But it's still you who's moving, and it's you who the prospect is buying. Do they trust you and like you? Do they believe you are an honest person of integrity that they should work with? Do they feel like they should follow you in this decision? If their answer is yes, they will buy from you, and if their answer is no, they won't. The key to making sure their answer is yes is to make sure you believe these things about yourself wholeheartedly, and your prospect will believe them about you. Sell yourself first, and you will sell the prospect successfully.

So the question becomes, how do you sell yourself, and the answer is by knowing who you are and why you do what you do. Knowing who you are is all about going inside and constantly working on yourself to be the best version of yourself you can possibly be—having a personal development plan that you do every day that brings out the best you possible—then putting that with everything else we've discussed in the previous chapter. Hence, you Sell on Purpose, and you sell yourself first.

You have to do the work! Years ago, I listened to a fantastic audio program by Zig Ziglar that talked about how what you do off the job has a significant impact on how well you do on the job. That is a perfect example of how important it is to have a personal development plan you do every day that brings out the best you possible. You are the key to your success, and you are your advantage in the marketplace. You can't be duplicated or copied! Your experiences, your personality, insights, and mindset are what set you apart. They are what make you unique, and that's what you should lead with to let your prospect know that these are the most important reasons to do business with you. When you Sell on Purpose, and you Sell yourself first, you eliminate all competition because no one can compete with you!

1. Do you have a personal development plan? ____________

____
____
____
____
____

2. If so, what is it? If not, why? ___________________________

____
____
____
____
____

3. If you don't have a personal development plan, write one down
    right now and commit to starting it today.____________

____
____
____
____
____
____
____
____
____

Chapter 5 - Influencing the Sale

Influence, what a great word! I love how it just rolls off the tongue and sounds so important. Influencing the sale to me means you have taken someone from interest to commitment. In my own sales career over the years, I've seen many strategies that my particular market has used to move prospects from interest to commitment. Most of which I have not personally been comfortable implementing into the way I wanted to do business. So, over time, I developed my own method that I felt good about! Years ago, when I started selling mortgage protection, which is a form of life insurance used to pay off the mortgage at the death of the insured. I was trained by my company to use tactics and pushy sales strategies to try and force the prospect into a buying decision. Being young and having minimal sales experience when I started, I followed their system and had some success. But over time, the more I read and developed myself, the more their way began to feel wrong to me. So I had to develop my own system of selling my product in a way that felt good to me on the inside. This is a key to selling successfully! You have to feel good on the inside and hold your integrity above all! What that means is you have to be honest with yourself and do what you know is right! You have to be able to look yourself in the mirror and feel good about all you did and said that day. Don't let anything come in between you and your integrity! No amount of money or status is worth your peace of mind and emotional well-being.

So I was trained to push people into buying, and over time I made changes to their system, which was more like pulling people into the decision. Pulling to me at that time felt a whole lot better than pushing, so that was my method of selling for the next few years. With more development and time, I began to create my own method of selling that I began to think of as persuading. Where pushing my prospect was all about trying to force them into a commitment without any information and using their need to make them commit prematurely, pulling was mostly the same thing but done in a less pushy way. Persuading, to me, was my way of becoming a consultant to my prospect. Instead of me mentally sitting across the table from them, I would move beside them and walk them through a process that helped them make the best decision for their family and loved ones! This way of selling felt the best to me and lined up with all of my beliefs and purpose.

I've never been money motivated, so I can't tell you I've made millions of dollars selling my product this way. My drive has always come from time freedom and exiting the rat race of which I have done through real estate investing. I set my own schedule and vacation when I want to, and as much as I want to, sometimes too much, but my success in selling was the key to my real estate investing. I tell you this not to impress you, but to impress upon you how important it is to find what drives you and use it.

So let's talk a little more about influencing the sale and how my method of persuasion works for me.

The first part of my persuasion process is the introduction. It's you introducing yourself to the prospect and getting to know them. F.O.R.M – Family, Occupation Recreation, and Message. Three question groups to get to know your prospect before giving them a message to begin the presentation. These three questions should be used with the intent to find out information that you will need to present your product or service in a way that will help you close the prospect. For example, if I'm selling a vacuum, and I begin by asking about their family dynamic. It's essential for me to gather information here to help me present and close my vacuum. Like how many kids? Then I could make a statement to see if they give more information to help me make my presentation like "wow, three kids, that's great. I grew up with three brothers, and our mom had a hard time keeping the carpet clean." They may let this statement pass by or it may open up a dialogue to express more pleasure or pain in that particular area. Both of which will be useful in the presentation and close.

The most important part of this process is for you to have one. A process that takes your prospect from interest to commitment no matter what you're selling. Then work on yourself and your sales process to make it better and better. Once I form a prospect, which is usually a 3-7 minute process, the next step is the presentation, which includes explaining information about the company, benefits of the product, showing the options, and then the close. Personally, I work in selling myself into the benefits of the product, and you should include it wherever it makes sense in your presentation as well.

Understand that your ability to influence the sale will include many factors, some totally out of your control, and some totally dependent on you. But what's important is to have a system and to work on it to make it better and better continuously. So your results will improve over time.

Tracking your activity and results is the key to making your results better. It will show you what's working and what's not. It will also show you how to increase your results and help you see inside your business. I have some free resources on my website that you can use to begin to track your activity and results if you don't already.

1. What is your sales process? _______________________________

____

____

____

____

____

____

2. Do you track your contacts, presentation, and sales? _____

____

____

____

____

____

____

3. If not, why not? ____

____

____

____

____

4. Do you know what your averages are?___________________

____

____

____

____

Chapter 6 - The power of belief

Do you believe you will be successful in sales and reach your goals? This question is so fundamental to your success and achievement of your individual goals for your business. Because as Henry Ford said, "Whether you think you can or you think you can't either way your right." So for all of the systems and processes that work, keep in mind that your individual results will be more of a self-fulfilling prophecy in the long run than the result of the system that you work day today. So it's essential for us to discuss the power of belief and how to increase it, thereby increasing your sales success.

Your belief in your own ability in every area of your life has its roots in your self-image. It's how you see yourself and who you believe yourself to be that has such a direct result on the outcome they tend to go hand and hand. For example, if you truly believe yourself to be a successful, goal-oriented person that eventually accomplishes your goals, you will put the time, energy, and effort into the accomplishment of your set goals. If you don't believe this about yourself, you won't set goals, and if you do set them as soon as you hit adversity, you will begin to look for excuses rather than ways to increase your results. And in life and business, we always eventually find what we're looking for. So my advice is to start with you! Start with the story you tell yourself about who you are and develop an empowering story that shows that you are who you want to be. Look at your past and find examples that support the belief you wish to live by. If you wish to believe yourself to be a winner, think about the times you have won in the past. Times you have pressed forward in the midst of uncertainty, and through continued action, you caused your dream to become a reality. No matter how big or small these successes matters, and they are evidence that you can set goals and achieve them. We all have a positive mental attitude, a mind that says we can and that we are well able. But we also carry a negative mental attitude that says we can't and that we are not capable or worthy. The key is to present evidence that supports your case and belief about yourself. Evidence that shows you're a winner and uses all the losses or times you haven't followed through as lessons of what not to do next time.

You have to believe in yourself and be your biggest supporter in the beginning, and eventually, others will come to replace you when they start to see your results.

Keep in mind that there are no unrealistic goals, just unrealistic time frames. You can achieve any goal, accomplish any dream, and fulfill any desire you are willing to invest the time, energy, and effort required. So set your goal, then decide what price you will have to pay to achieve it and get busy paying that price! If at any time you find it hard to believe your goals, dreams, and desires are achievable, just remind yourself that they're possible. It's possible for you to win! You can prosper! You can succeed beyond your wildest dreams if you continue to invest your time, energy, and effort towards your desired outcome. Some goals you will be able to accomplish faster than you initially thought possible, and others will take longer than you can presently imagine, so always make sure your aim is worthy of your pursuit. A worthy goal, when accomplished, not only brings you what you desire, but it also should turn you into a better person than you currently are! So make sure your goal is worthy of you and your purpose.

1. On a scale of 1-10 1 being you have an extremely low self-image and 10 being you can't imagine it being any higher, where do you fall and why?________________________

____

____

____

____

2. What story have you been telling yourself about what's possible for you?________________________________

____

____

____

____

____

____

____

____

____

____

____

____

3. Is this story helping you achieve your goals, dreams, and desires? If not, how can you change your story to help you instead of allowing it to hinder you?__________________

____

____

____

____

____

____

____

____

____

____

____

Chapter 7 - Sales Significance (survival, stability, success, and significance)

In my opinion, your sales career will have four stages of development, each stage requiring different skills to move to the next level of advancement. When we're new to sales, we all start out in sales survival; in this stage, we don't know what we don't know, and we're at the mercy of our company or trainer to show us the way. We're so new that anxiety and stress plague us during our prospecting and presentations. We're uncertain, fearful, and we constantly question ourselves, wondering if this new venture will work for us. It's in this stage that most quit and go back to their previous occupation. The key to moving to the next stage is to understand that sales is a numbers game and to work the numbers in your favor, and then you will move from survival to stability.

The next stage is sales stability; it's this stage that you begin to understand that sales is a numbers game, and you begin to work those numbers to your benefit. It's here that you have bought into your ability to sell, and you begin to understand your prospect and yourself. Your results start to come consistently, and you begin to envision higher levels of success and accomplishment. But to move from stability to success, you must pass the persistence test. When you are stable, but you want to grow and achieve more, it's here where you begin to form a new foundation. This stage requires persistence and will require you to be consistent in your actions and when you have wholeheartedly decided to continue no matter what you will then and only then move to the next stage, which is sales success.

Welcome to sales success, it's at this stage that you have mastered the basics, and you fully understand what's required to achieve the results you want. You also Sell on Purpose, and you have accomplished many, if not all, the goals you have set for yourself. Then you begin to wonder what else is there and what's next for you. You start to look for new meaning and fulfillment in your profession. New goals start to lose their pull, and your desires just don't push you like they used to. Finally, you begin to look outside of yourself to see who you can bring along with you and who you can help to get to where you're at. These thoughts and actions lead you into sales significance!

Sales significance is where you Sell on Purpose, and you show others how to do the same! It's not about you anymore, and now your goals are aligned with you helping others to reach theirs! You genuinely want to see others win, and you're excited about their victories just as much as you were excited for your own. You're now a coach and a developer. You understand each stage and what's required to move to the next one. But most importantly, you know that without constant action, stability can backslide to survival and success can quickly turn into sales stability as well. You have probably moved to and from each stage through your years in sales, and it's these experiences that will help those who have joined you to accomplish their goals, dreams, and desires.

You see, it's what we give that truly gives us our meaning and purpose! It's when we pour ourselves out that we begin to be filled. Hopefully, this book has filled you with some ideas and insights that you can use to achieve more and go further. Thank you for investing your time learning how to Sell on Purpose, and I wish you all the success you can imagine...

1. What stage are you in? (Sales Survival, Sales Stability, Sales Success, or Sales Significance)?______________

____

____

____

____

2. What do you need to do in order to move from where you are to where you want to go?________

____

____

____

____

____

____

____

3. Set the date for when you will reach that goal and make a list of all the actions you need to take in order to accomplish your goal. __________________

____

____

____

____

____

____

____

____

____

____

4. Break your goal down in stages and set a target date
    for each stage that leads to the final date that you
    have set. ___________________________________

    ____

    ____

    ____

    ____

    ____

    ____

    ____

    ____

    ____

    ____

    ____

    ____

    ____

5. Today's Date is   / / / , which is the day I will begin
    to take the actions necessary for me to accomplish
    my goals.

About The Author

Lamar Skipper is the Owner & Founder of Work Smarter Insurance & Quality Insurance LLC based in Toledo, Ohio. Lamar loves to help agents work smarter so they can leverage their time, energy, and effort while helping more people in less time!

Lamar believes that personal and professional development is the key to reaching higher and higher levels of success. He is also a student of human potential and loves to help people achieve their goals, dreams, and desires. Connect with Lamar on youtube.com/user/lamarskipper,

www.LamarSkipper.com,

or www.BooksByLamarSkipper.com